THE

MAYO CLINIC

COOKBOOK FOR BEGINNERS

Over 120 Delicious Mayo Clinic Diet Recipes
for Total Body Transformation and Weight
Loss.

Written and Edited by
Louisa Vonnegut

Table of Contents

INTRODUCTION..1

The Mayo Clinic Diet: What Is It? 4

The Mayo Clinic Diet Approach: An Overview..7

Phases and Duration 11

Can It Help You Lose Weight? 13

Macronutrients and Micronutrients: Nutritional Fundamentals 15

What advantages does the Mayo Clinic diet offer? 19

Portion Control: A Mayo Clinic Diet Key to Balanced Eating 21

The 7-day Mayo Clinic Diet Meal Plan 25

What You Can Eat 27

What You Cannot Eat 29

How to Prepare the Mayo Clinic Diet and Tips? 30

Sample Shopping List...................................32

Pros of the Mayo Clinic Diet 34

Cons of the Mayo Clinic Diet.........................36

Is the Mayo Clinic Diet a Healthy Choices for You?..38

Recipes for Mayo Clinic Diet............................39

Asian Pork Tenderloin...............................39

Asparagus, Tomato and Red Pepper French
Bread Pizza 40

Baked Blueberry French Toast.......................42

Baked Chicken and Wild Rice with Onions
Tarragon..43

Baked Cod with Lemon and Capers...............45

Baked Macaroni with Red Sauce...................46

Baked Oatmeal..48

Baked Salmon with Southeast Asian Marinade
....49

Baked Zitti with Vegetables 50

Balsamic Feta Chicken..................................53

Balsamic Roast Chicken 54

Barbecue Chicken Pizza...............................56

Barbecued Pork Tenderloin 57

Almond Crusted Chicken.............................59

6-Grain Hot Cereal...................................... 61

Barley and Roasted Tomato Risotto..............62

Bean Saled with Balsamic Vinaigrette...........65

Beef and Vegetable Kebabs...........................66

Beef and Vegetable Stew 68

Beef Fajitas 70

Beef Stew with Fennel and Shallots............... 71

Beef Stroganoff 74

Black Bean Burgers with Chipotle Ketchup 76

CONCLUSION 80

INTRODUCTION

Welcome to "The Optimal Mayo Clinic Cookbook for Beginners," a culinary adventure that combines the art of excellent cooking with the science of wellbeing. When you open this book, you're not just getting a collection of recipes; you're also learning how to embrace a lifestyle influenced by the famed Mayo Clinic diet.

Have you ever considered that healthy eating may be a fascinating symphony of flavors? Prepare to be blown away as I lead you through a treasure trove of 100 expertly designed meals that highlight the freshness of fresh ingredients. From scrumptious breakfasts that wake you up with a surge of energy to filling meals that give the day a delightful farewell, each dish offers a story of sustenance and happiness.

This book, however, is more than just recipes. It's your guide on the path to greater health. Let's deconstruct the Mayo Clinic diet together, breaking it down into simple, daily choices. With my help, you'll not only comprehend the "what" and "why" of this method, but you'll also be able to seamlessly incorporate its essence into your culinary story.

And if structure is important to you, I've got you covered. Explore our carefully chosen 7-day meal plan, which serves as a road map for your gastronomic adventure throughout the week. Say goodbye to the perplexity of knowing what to eat and when, and welcome to a fresh harmony between your taste sensations and your health goals.

So, whether you're a newbie in the kitchen looking to start a healthy lifestyle or a seasoned cook looking to infuse your meals with a new sense of purpose, "The Optimal Mayo Clinic Cookbook for Beginners" offers a journey that will satisfy both your palate and your curiosity. Let us go on this journey of flavor, education, and wellbeing together, one delicious recipe at a time.

The Mayo Clinic Diet: What Is It?

The Mayo Clinic Diet, which beat out Jenny Craig and Noom, has been designated one of the best diets of 2021 by a panel of analysts and medical professionals at U.S. News & World Report. Given that the plan doesn't have a rigid set of rules, its current rating as the second-best paid weight reduction program could come as a surprise, especially to individuals who are considering following popular diets in the New Year that frequently eliminate whole food groups.

The Mayo Clinic Diet, which emphasizes time-tested nutritional recommendations in a fresh approach, instead zeroes emphasis on the medical center's iconic food pyramid.

The Mayo Clinic Diet focuses on changing any unhealthy eating patterns and increasing consumption of whole-grain, fruit, and vegetable mainstays, as well as boosted protein and the occasional sweet indulgence. The Mayo Clinic Diet promises quick effects in the first two weeks of the program by encouraging you to eat more vegetables, fruits, and grains high in fiber and other nutrients:

According to the program's website, weight loss can range from 5 to 10 pounds. The diet's real appeal, though, may lie in the fact that it is designed to last longer than these two weeks, with a phase that encourages two pounds of weight reduction every week until you've reached your target weight. The Mayo Clinic Diet may technically be followed for as long as you'd want, and some dieters choose to follow its guidelines for the rest of their lives.

The diet calls for you to consume fewer calories than usual as little as 1,200 for women and 1,400 for men for the first two weeks but it doesn't urge you to completely give up bread or never eat dessert.

The Mayo Clinic Diet Approach: An Overview

The Mayo Clinic Diet is a weight reduction and healthy lifestyle diet established by doctors at the famous Mayo Clinic. It is vital to distinguish the Mayo Clinic Diet from the "Mayo Clinic Fad Diet," which is not approved by the clinic and has been linked to incorrect information.

The Mayo Clinic Diet method focuses on long-term weight control by combining a balanced and nutritious eating plan with physical exercise and behavioral modification. The following are the main concepts of the Mayo Clinic Diet:

- **Healthy Eating Habits:** The Mayo Clinic Diet stresses adopting long-term healthy eating choices. It promotes the eating of entire foods such as fruits and vegetables, lean proteins, whole grains, and healthy fats while restricting the consumption of processed meals, sugary snacks, and excessive amounts of refined carbs.

- **Portion management:** Portion management is an important part of diet. To avoid overeating and to help regulate calorie consumption, the Mayo Clinic Diet advises you to be conscious of portion sizes.

- **Fruits and vegetables:** The diet emphasizes fruits and vegetables, which are high in vitamins, minerals, and fiber. These meals can help you feel full and satisfied while also helping you control your calorie consumption.

- **Physical exercise:** A fundamental component of the Mayo Clinic Diet is regular physical exercise. It encourages you to include exercise into your everyday routine to help you lose weight and improve your overall health.

- **Changes in Lifestyle:** The Mayo Clinic Diet recognizes the importance of behavioral modification in obtaining and maintaining a healthy weight. It encourages you to create realistic objectives, develop beneficial habits, and make long-term adjustments to your daily routine.

- **Breakfast Importance:** The diet emphasizes starting the day with a healthy and balanced breakfast. A good breakfast can provide you energy for the day and help you avoid overeating later.

- **Snacking Wisely:** To help decrease hunger between meals, the Mayo Clinic Diet advises mindful snacking on nutritious foods such as fruits, vegetables, almonds, and yogurt.

- **Hydration:** Staying hydrated is important for general health and can help with weight reduction. Water and other non-caloric liquids are encouraged to be consumed.

- **Slow and Steady Weight Loss:** The Mayo Clinic Diet promotes progressive and sustainable weight loss as opposed to severe or quick methods. It strives for a consistent and reasonable weight reduction rate of 1 to 2 pounds each week.

- **Support and Accountability:** The Mayo Clinic Diet values both support and accountability. Connecting with people who are adopting healthy lifestyle changes might assist you in staying motivated and on track.

It is crucial to know that the Mayo Clinic Diet is established by medical specialists and is based on evidence-based procedures. Individual outcomes may vary, so talk with a healthcare physician before beginning any new diet or weight reduction program, especially if you have any underlying health concerns.

There are two phases in the Mayo Clinic Diet:

- **Lose it!** The first two weeks are designed to jumpstart your weight loss.
- **Live it!** The second phase is meant to be followed for life.

The first phase of the diet focuses on 15 habits: 5 you should break, 5 new habits you should form, and 5 bonus habits to optimize your results.

You're encouraged to do the following to break certain habits:
- Avoid eating added sugar.
- Refrain from snacking, except for fruits and vegetables.
- Don't eat too much meat and full fat dairy.
- Never eat while watching TV.
- Avoid eating out — unless the food you order follows the diet's rules.

You're advised to develop these habits:

- Eat a healthy breakfast.
- Consume at least four servings of vegetables and fruits per day.
- Eat whole grains like brown rice and barley.
- Focus on healthy fats like olive oil, while limiting saturated fats and avoid trans fats.
- Walk or exercise for 30 minutes or more every day.

Bonus habits to adopt include keeping food and activity journals, exercising for 60 minutes or more per day, and avoiding processed foods.

Can It Help You Lose Weight?

The Mayo Clinic Diet may help you lose weight for several reasons.

It encourages exercise alongside a nutritious diet of fruits, vegetables, and whole grains all of which may aid weight loss.

Eating foods high in fiber may boost weight loss by decreasing hunger and making you feel full for a longer period of time.

In one study involving over 3,000 people at risks for diabetes, a diet high in fiber from fruits and vegetables and low in saturated fat was linked to a lower weight after 1 year compared to people who did not increase their fiber intake.

Additionally, studies show that exercising while on a lower calorie diet is more effective at promoting weight loss than dieting alone.

For example, a review of 66 studies found that combining low calorie diets with exercise especially resistance training is more effective at promoting weight and fat loss than dieting alone.

Plus, simultaneous dieting and exercise helps retain more muscle mass, which could further promote weight loss by boosting metabolism.

The only research on the Mayo Clinic Diet comes from the Mayo Clinic itself and has not been published in a peer-reviewed journal.

Thus, no independent studies exist on the effectiveness of the Mayo Clinic Diet.
More research is necessary to determine whether it's effective for weight loss.

Macronutrients and Micronutrients: Nutritional Fundamentals

Think of your body as a well-tuned machine that needs a variety of things to operate at its optimal level. Your body requires nutrition to thrive, much like a car needs fuel to run. The two primary groups of these nutrients are macronutrients and micronutrients, each of which is essential for preserving your health.

Macronutrients: Fuel for Your Body's Engine

The main source of energy your body needs to function effectively is provided by macronutrients. Because your body needs them in greater quantities than micronutrients, they are referred to as "macro" nutrients. The three main macronutrients are:

✓ **Carbohydrates:** These are your body's primary source of energy. Think of them as your engine's premium fuels. Foods include grains (bread, rice, and pasta), fruits, vegetables, and legumes all contain carbohydrates. Your cells utilize the glucose that results from their breakdown as fuel.

✓ **Proteins:** Think of proteins as your body's building blocks. They are necessary for manufacturing enzymes and hormones as well as for repairing and constructing tissues. Think of them as the laborers who are renovating and constructing new buildings in your body. Lean meats, poultry, fish, beans, nuts, and dairy products are all excellent sources of protein.

✓ **Fats:** Although they frequently have a poor name, fats are essential for many biological processes. Consider them to be the lubricant that keeps your machine in good working order. Fats are necessary for cell structure, energy production, and the absorption of fat-soluble vitamins (more on this later). Avocados, almonds, seeds, olive oil, and fatty seafood are all good sources of fat.

Micronutrients: The Little Helpers

Micronutrients are equally as important as macronutrients, despite the fact that you require them in lesser amounts. Although these nutrients don't directly produce energy, they are essential to many physiological functions. Micronutrients include:

✓ **Vitamins:** These are like the tiny tools your body uses to perform specific tasks. Vitamins are necessary for a number of processes, including enhancing your immune system (vitamin C), maintaining bone health (vitamin D), and encouraging good vision. Numerous fruits, vegetables, and fortified meals include vitamins.

Minerals: Your body's structure is built on a foundation of minerals. They have a role in processes including bone health, fluid balance, and nerve function. Calcium, iron, magnesium, and potassium are a few minerals. Minerals are abundant in foods like dairy products, leafy greens, whole grains, and lean meats.

A balanced diet is emphasized by the Mayo Clinic Diet. It advises you to put your attention on entire, nutrient-dense foods that offer a variety of macronutrients and micronutrients. You can make sure your body receives the macronutrients and micronutrients it needs to function well by include a range of foods in your diet.

What advantages does the Mayo Clinic diet offer?

Maintains heart health
The Mayo Clinic diet places a strong focus on fruits, vegetables, and whole grains as a fundamental tenet. These foods include a lot of dietary fiber, which controls cholesterol levels and improves general heart health, reducing the risk of heart disease.

Encourages weight loss
The Mayo Clinic diet promotes balanced, portion-controlled eating, which can help with weight loss. It is based on the food pyramid, which places an emphasis on nutritious grains, fruits, and vegetables above fats and sweets to help create a calorie deficit without sacrificing important nutrients.

Wellness of the digestive system
The Mayo Clinic diet supports a strong and effective digestive tract because it places a strong emphasis on whole foods and dietary fiber. You

may stay away from issues like constipation, bloating, and irritable bowel syndrome by having regular and proper digestion. Find out which foods are the highest in fiber.

Promotes leading a healthy lifestyle

The diet aims for more than just weight loss. Long-term practices that can lead to a healthy lifestyle are introduced and reinforced. This also offers advice on mindful eating and frequent exercise.

Portion Control: A Mayo Clinic Diet Key to Balanced Eating

The Mayo Clinic Diet places a strong emphasis on portion management, which stresses consuming the proper quantity of food to develop balanced and healthy eating habits. It is crucial for sustaining a healthy weight and fostering general wellbeing.

Instead than adhering to fad diets or severe limitations, the Mayo Clinic Diet concentrates on helping people make long-lasting adjustments to their eating patterns. A crucial idea in calorie management is portion control, which helps people avoid overeating, which can result in weight gain and other health problems.

The Mayo Clinic Diet's portion management guidelines are broken out as follows:

✓ **Understanding Serving Sizes:** Because they are unsure of what constitutes an appropriate serving size, many people overestimate the quantity of food they consume. The Mayo Clinic Diet advises people to get familiar with the suggested serving sizes for several dietary groups, including grains, proteins, vegetables, and fruits. By being mindful, one may avoid consuming too many calories.

✓ **Balanced Meals:** Portion control goes beyond just limiting how much food you consume. Additionally, well-balanced meals with a range of nutrient-dense foods must be prepared. People may eat a variety of fruits and vegetables, whole grains, healthy fats, and lean meats to feel full while also feeding their bodies.

✓ **Mindful Eating:** The Mayo Clinic Diet emphasizes mindful eating, which involves being fully present during meals and paying attention to hunger and fullness cues. Slowing down and enjoying each meal might help you avoid overeating since it allows your body time to let you know when it is full.

✓ **Utilizing Tools:** Using portion control tools can help you regulate your calorie consumption. By using smaller bowls, plates, and utensils, you may persuade your brain that you are eating a greater piece. Accurate meal portioning can also be aided by measuring cups and food scales.

✓ **Keeping Away from Emotional Eating:** The Mayo Clinic Diet understands the need of managing emotional eating habits. Food is frequently used as a comfort or coping mechanism by people. Making better decisions and avoiding overeating can be accomplished by learning to distinguish between actual hunger and emotional cues.

✓ **Planning ahead:** Making informed decisions regarding portion sizes can be aided by scheduling meals and snacks in advance. When you have a plan, it's less likely that you'll pick for bad foods or eat more since it's easier.

✓ **Listening to Your Body:** The Mayo Clinic Diet encourages individuals to listen to their bodies and eat when they're hungry, stopping when they're comfortably full. This behavior promotes a better connection with food and prevents the sensation of being overstuffed.

You may lose weight or maintain your current weight by incorporating portion management techniques into your eating routine.

The 7-day Mayo Clinic Diet Meal Plan

The New Mayo Clinic Diet focuses on eating nutritious foods that are filling, with unlimited vegetables and fruits on the menu. Utilizing a tier program, the diet suggests eating the majority of foods from the base and reducing your intake as you move toward the top tier.

- ✓ **Base tier:** Fruits and vegetables
- ✓ **Second tier:** Whole grain carbohydrates
- ✓ **Third tier:** Lean protein, such as fish, chicken, legumes, and low-fat dairy
- ✓ **Fourth tier:** Healthy fats like nuts and avocados
- ✓ **Fifth tier:** Sweets are not off-limit, but should fit into your daily calorie intake without replacing foods on the lower tiers.

Given the program's flexibility, you have plenty of room to create a variety of meals for all tastes and dietary requirements. Remember, fruit and vegetables are unlimited and are ideal as snacks.

Here is a 7-day sample menu, some of which comes directly from the Mayo Clinic's library of meals.

- **Day 1:** Breakfast burrito, rice salad, Thai-inspired pork with quinoa
- **Day 2:** Pancakes with blueberries, tuna salad pita, whole-grain spaghetti with homemade sauce
- **Day 3:** Baked eggs and beans, poke bowl, chicken curry
- **Day 4:** Whole-grain cereal, grilled chicken salad, grilled tuna with brown rice and vegetables
- **Day 5:** Oatmeal with raisins, quinoa and sweet potato cakes, rosemary lemon chicken
- **Day 6:** Ricotta and tomato wrap, buddha bowl, lentil, and tofu curry
- **Day 7:** Whole-wheat tortilla with vegetables and low-fat cheese, mixed bean salad, mango salad pizza

What You Can Eat

As outlined above, the Mayo Clinic Diet is an approach to eating nutritious whole foods incorporated into nutrient-based meals, for a slow and steady approach to weight management. No foods are strictly off-limits.

Fruits and vegetables
Fruits and vegetables should form the basis of your diet in the Mayo Clinic Diet and are encouraged in abundance.

Complex Carbohydrates
Staples such as whole-wheat bread and pasta, and brown rice, alongside quinoa, beans, lentils, and other whole grains are encouraged. In general, choose complex carbohydrates like whole grains over refined carbs like white bread, as they are more nutrient-dense and higher in fiber which will help keep you feeling full longer.

Protein
Lean meats, chicken, fish, nuts, beans are good choices of protein in the diet.

Fats
Gear your fat intake toward unsaturated options, including olive oil, nuts, fish, avocados, and chia seeds. Unsaturated fat can improve your cholesterol levels and also reduce the risk of coronary heart disease.

Sweets
Although not prohibited, sugar disrupts your blood sugar control. Therefore, sweet foods should be consumed in moderation.

What You Cannot Eat

There are no restricted foods on the diet, although alcohol and foods with added sugar are not allowed during the 2-week "Lose It" phase. The least amount of calories should be dedicated to sweets, at around 75 calories a day.

If you have diabetes, you may need to limit fruit or select low-sugar options because of the natural sugars. Talk to a healthcare provider or registered dietitian for input on what is right for you.

How to Prepare the Mayo Clinic Diet and Tips?

Similar to other diets, much of the success lies in how you prepare. Make sure to do your research prior to starting and stock up on permitted foods, clearing your fridge and cupboards of highly processed, sugary foods that can lead to temptation.

Once your initial shopping list and meals are planned, the program starts with the "Lose It" phase, in which might see an initial 6- to 10-pound weight loss. Keep in mind, this number is not necessarily reflective of fat loss, rather more likely a combination of fat, muscle, and water weight.

The "Lose It" phase is a transition period that teaches you to adopt new eating habits and will continue to guide your diet during the Live It phase. Here, you might see a weekly weight loss of around 1 to 2 pounds. Remember, studies have found the key to weight loss success is in implementing long-term lifestyle changes, so it is wiser to lose weight gradually.

A few resources are available from the Mayo Clinic, including "The Optimal Mayo Clinic Cookbook for Beginners" and accompanying journal to plan and track your meals and progress. There is also an online program that starts at $4.61 a week, featuring meal ideas, recipes, apps, trackers, virtual video group sessions, and practical workouts.

The Mayo Clinic also offers "The Mayo Clinic Diabetes Diet" book for people with pre-diabetes and type 2 diabetes. As with any weight-loss program, you should discuss the plan with a healthcare provider prior to starting, especially if you have diabetes or another health condition.

Sample Shopping List

There is a bounty of foods included in the Mayo Diet Clinic. Many are encouraged in high volume, while others, although not restricted, should be limited. The following sample shopping list is a guide to get you started:

- Dark leafy greens (spinach, kale, arugula, Swiss chard, collard greens, bok choy)
- Vegetables (broccoli, cauliflower, Brussels sprouts, bell peppers, eggplant, carrots)
- Fresh and frozen fruits (grapefruit, oranges, berries, bananas, apples)
- Whole grains (quinoa, barley, amaranth, brown rice, sourdough, 12-grain bread)
- Legumes (black beans, lentils, chickpeas, tofu)
- Meat and poultry (lean ground beef, chicken, turkey breast)
- Fresh or frozen fish (halibut, cod, salmon, snapper, sea bass, shrimp)
- Eggs
- Low-fat dairy products (feta cheese, Greek yogurt, cottage cheese)

- Healthy fats (avocados, walnuts, almonds, chia seeds, olive oil)

Pros of the Mayo Clinic Diet

The Mayo Clinic Diet has been researched and designed under the guidance of weight-management experts and is, therefore, likely to be safe and effective for most people. To achieve the desired results, you must adhere to the plan fully, which may require determination, a change in mindset, and a willingness to succeed.

Here are some of the diet's pros:

✓ **Provides nutrient-dense foods:** The Mayo Clinic Diet's food pyramid reflects solid nutrition standards and recommendations for centering your diet around nutritious, energy-boosting foods. The limit placed on sweets and highly-processed foods encourages nutritious eating regardless of whether your goal is weight management or not.

✓ **Includes an exercise component:** Thirty minutes of daily activity is recommended as part of the program. It is incorporated at the base of the tier system, highlighting the importance of exercise and wellness in your weight management goals. It also teaches you to establish new habits and goals.

✓ **Promotes long-term success:** Rather than a quick fix, the Mayo Clinic Diet is intended to overhaul your lifestyle with optimal habits that will stick in the long term. Therefore, rather than yo-yo dieting, you can achieve realistic weight management goals.

Cons of the Mayo Clinic Diet

As with most diets, there is no guarantee of its suitability for your lifestyle and caloric needs. As such, the Mayo Clinic Diet has a few cons to consider:

May feel restrictive initially: The Lose It phase is restrictive in terms of cutting out processed sugar, alcohol, and even eating out. While there are no common risks associated with the Mayo Clinic Diet, some people may find it difficult to meet all of their nutritional needs during the restrictive weight-loss phase of the plan.

Can be time-consuming: Eating a lot of fruits and vegetables, and avoiding refined or processed foods, will take time and effort. Overall, you will adopt new ways of grocery shopping, planning meals, and cooking.

Requires a low-calorie intake: While the recommended 1,200-1,400 calories (if you weigh 250 pounds or less) might be sufficient for some, this number may be too low if you live a particularly active lifestyle, or, for example, are tall and, therefore, require additional calories. You need to ensure you are sufficiently fueling your body for exercise and daily energy stores. Otherwise, you may find the diet ineffective in the long term for weight maintenance.

In general, you should not be following a diet plan under 1,200 calories, unless under special circumstances. Such a low-caloric intake can be detrimental to your health as you can become deficient in certain nutrients, and therefore not optimally fuel your body with the energy it needs.

Is the Mayo Clinic Diet a Healthy Choices for You?

The real Mayo Clinic Diet is similar to other nutritious eating patterns that emphasize lifelong strategies for eating and follow many of the federal dietary guidelines set forth in the U.S. Department of Agriculture's 2020–2025 Dietary Guidelines for Americans. As such, the diet encourages a variety of nutrient-dense foods without restricting what foods are included in the diet.

If you prefer to follow a guided eating plan and lifestyle guidance, you might find benefit in the Mayo Clinic Diet. However, given that it recommends a target calorie range of between 1,200-1,800 calories, depending on your sex and weight, you need to ensure it is a suitable fit for your energy needs. A weight-loss calculator can be used to determine a daily calorie target to meet your goals.

Recipes for Mayo Clinic Diet

Asian Pork Tenderloin

Ingredients
- 2 tablespoons sesame seeds
- 1 teaspoon ground coriander
- 1/8 teaspoon cayenne pepper
- 1/8 teaspoon celery seed
- 1/2 teaspoon minced onion
- 1/4 teaspoon ground cumin
- 1/8 teaspoon ground cinnamon
- 1 tablespoon sesame oil
- 1 pound pork tenderloin, sliced into 4 portions

Directions
- Heat the oven to 400 F.
- Lightly coat a baking dish with cooking spray.
- In a heavy frying pan, add the sesame seeds in a single layer.
- Over low heat, cook the seeds, stirring constantly until they look golden and give

off a noticeably toasty aroma, about 1 to 2 minutes.

- Remove the seeds from the pan to cool.
- In a bowl, add the coriander, cayenne pepper, celery seed, minced onion, cumin, cinnamon, sesame oil and toasted sesame seeds.
- Stir to mix evenly.
- Place the pork tenderloin in the prepared baking dish.
- Rub the spices on both sides of the pork pieces.
- Bake until no longer pink, about 15 minutes.
- Or bake until a meat thermometer reaches 165 F (medium) or 170 F (well-done).

Asparagus, Tomato and Red Pepper French Bread Pizza

Ingredients
- 1 cup diced asparagus
- 1 cup diced Roma tomatoes
- 1 cup diced red bell pepper
- 1 tablespoon minced garlic

- 1 loaf French bread, about 8 inches long, sliced in half and cut into 4-inch sections
- 1 cup pizza sauce
- 1 cup reduced-fat shredded mozzarella cheese

Directions
- Heat the oven to 400 F.
- Lightly coat a baking sheet with cooking spray.
- In a small bowl, add the asparagus, tomatoes and pepper.
- Add the garlic and toss gently to coat evenly.
- Arrange the French bread on the baking sheet.
- Add 1/4 cup of the pizza sauce and 1/4 of the vegetable mixture to each section.
- Sprinkle each with 1/4 cup mozzarella cheese.
- Bake until the cheese is lightly browned and the vegetables are tender, about 8 to 10 minutes.
- Serve immediately.

Baked Blueberry French Toast

Ingredients
- 12-inch French or sourdough baguette
- 4 egg whites
- 1 cup fat-free soy milk
- 1/4 teaspoon nutmeg
- 1 teaspoon vanilla
- 4 tablespoons brown sugar, divided
- 3/4 cup blueberries, coarsely chopped
- 1 tablespoon canola oil
- 1/4 cup chopped pecans, toasted (optional; not included in the nutritional analysis)

Directions
- Spray a 9-inch square baking dish with cooking spray.
- Cut 10 1-inch-thick slices from baguette.
- Arrange in baking dish.
- In a large bowl, whisk egg whites until frothy.
- Then whisk in milk, nutmeg, vanilla and 2 tablespoons brown sugar.
- Pour evenly over bread, turning slices to coat evenly.

- Cover pan.
- Chill at least 8 hours or overnight, until liquid is absorbed by bread.
- Heat oven to 400 F.
- Drop blueberries evenly over bread.
- In a small bowl, stir together 2 tablespoons brown sugar and oil, and pecans if you wish.
- Spoon evenly over bread.
- Bake, uncovered, about 20 minutes, until liquid from blueberries is bubbling.

Baked Chicken and Wild Rice with Onions Tarragon

Ingredients
- 1 pound boneless, skinless chicken breast halves
- 1 1/2 cups chopped celery
- 1 1/2 cups whole pearl onions
- 1 teaspoon fresh tarragon
- 2 cups unsalted chicken broth
- 3/4 cup uncooked long-grain white rice
- 3/4 cup uncooked wild rice
- 1 1/2 cups dry white wine

Directions

- Heat the oven to 300 F.
- Cut chicken breasts into 1-inch pieces. In a nonstick frying pan, combine the chicken, celery, onions and tarragon with 1 cup of the unsalted chicken broth.
- Cook on medium heat until the chicken and vegetables are tender, about 10 minutes. Set aside to cool.
- In a baking dish, stir together the rice, wine and remaining 1 cup chicken broth.
- Let soak for 30 minutes.
- Add the chicken and vegetables to the baking dish.
- Cover and bake for 60 minutes.
- Check periodically and add more broth if the rice is too dry.
- Serve immediately.

Baked Cod with Lemon and Capers

Ingredients
- 4 cod fillets, each 6 ounces
- 1 lemon
- 1 teaspoon low-sodium chicken-flavored bouillon granules
- 1 cup hot tap water
- 1 tablespoon butter, softened
- 1 tablespoon all-purpose flour
- 4 teaspoons capers, rinsed and drained

Directions
- Heat the oven to 350 F.
- Spray 4 squares of foil with cooking spray.
- Place 1 cod fillet on each foil square.
- Cut lemon in half.
- Squeeze the juice from one half over the fish.
- Cut the other half into slices, place over the fish and seal the foil.
- Bake in the oven until the fish is opaque throughout when tested with the tip of a knife, about 20 minutes.

- In a small bowl, add the chicken bouillon granules and the hot tap water.
- Stir until the granules dissolve.
- Set aside.
- In another small bowl, mix the butter and flour together.
- Transfer to a heavy saucepan.
- Stir over moderate heat until the butter-flour mixture melts.
- Add the bouillon to the butter mixture and continue to stir until thickened.
- Add the capers and remove from the heat.
- Pour over the fish and serve.

Baked Macaroni with Red Sauce

Ingredients
- 1/2 pound extra-lean ground beef
- 1 small onion, diced (about 1/2 cup)
- 1 box (7 ounces) whole-wheat elbow macaroni
- 1 jar (15 ounces) reduced-sodium spaghetti sauce, 6 tablespoons Parmesan cheese

Directions

- Heat the oven to 350 F.
- Lightly coat a baking dish with cooking spray.
- In a nonstick frying pan, cook ground beef and onion until the meat is browned and the onion is translucent.
- Drain well and set aside.
- Fill a large pot 3/4 full with water and bring to a boil.
- Add the pasta and cook until al dente, 10 to 12 minutes, or according to the package directions.
- Drain the pasta thoroughly.
- Add the cooked pasta and spaghetti sauce to the meat and onions.
- Stir to mix evenly.
- Spoon the mixture into the prepared baking dish.
- Bake until bubbly, about 25 to 35 minutes.
- Divide the macaroni among individual plates.
- Sprinkle each with 1 tablespoon Parmesan cheese.
- Serve immediately.

Baked Oatmeal

Ingredients
- 1 tablespoon canola oil
- 1/2 cup unsweetened applesauce
- 1/3 cup brown sugar
- Egg substitute equivalent to 2 eggs, or 4 egg whites
- 3 cups uncooked rolled oats
- 2 teaspoons baking powder
- 1 teaspoon cinnamon
- 1 cup skim milk

Directions
- In a good-sized bowl, stir together oil, applesauce, sugar and eggs.
- Add dry ingredients and milk.
- Mix well.
- Spray a 9-by-13 baking pan generously with cooking spray.
- Spoon oatmeal mixture into pan.
- Bake uncovered at 350 F for 30 minutes.

Baked Salmon with Southeast Asian Marinade

Ingredients
- 1/2 cup pineapple juice (no sugar added)
- 2 garlic cloves, minced
- 1 teaspoon low-sodium soy sauce
- 1/4 teaspoon ground ginger
- 2 salmon fillets, each 4 ounces
- 1/4 teaspoon sesame oil
- Freshly ground black pepper, to taste
- 1 cup diced fresh fruit, such as pineapple, mango and papaya

Directions
- In a small bowl, add the pineapple juice, garlic, soy sauce and ginger.
- Stir to mix evenly.
- Arrange the salmon fillets in a small baking dish.
- Pour the pineapple juice mixture over the top.
- Put in the refrigerator and marinate for 1 hour.
- Turn the salmon periodically as needed.
- Heat the oven to 375 F.

- Lightly coat 2 squares of aluminum foil with cooking spray.
- Place the marinated salmon fillets on the aluminum foil.
- Drizzle each with 1/8 teaspoon sesame oil.
- Sprinkle with pepper and top each with 1/2 cup diced fruit.
- Wrap the foil around the salmon, folding the edges to seal.
- Bake until the fish is opaque throughout when tested with the tip of a knife, about 10 minutes on each side.
- Transfer the salmon to warmed individual plates and serve immediately.

Baked Zitti with Vegetables

Ingredients
- 2/3 cup uncooked ziti (about 2 ounces)
- 1 can (14 ounces) low-sodium tomatoes, drained (reserve 1/2 cup of the juice)
- 1/2 cup sliced carrots
- 1 cup chopped broccoli
- 1/2 cup diced green bell pepper
- 1/4 cup sliced mushrooms

- 2 garlic cloves, minced
- 1 teaspoon dried basil
- 1 teaspoon dried oregano
- 1/2 teaspoon ground black pepper
- 1/2 cup reduced-fat shredded mozzarella cheese
- 1/2 cup grated Parmesan cheese

Directions

- Heat the oven to 375 F.
- Lightly coat a baking dish with cooking spray.
- Fill a large pot 3/4 full with water and bring to a boil.
- Add the pasta and cook until al dente (tender), 10 to 12 minutes, or according to the package directions.
- Drain the pasta thoroughly.
- In a nonstick frying pan over medium heat, add the reserved juice from the canned tomatoes.
- Stir in the carrots, broccoli and green pepper.
- Saute the vegetables until tender, about 5 minutes.

- Add the mushrooms and garlic and cook for another 5 minutes.
- Add the tomatoes, basil, oregano and black pepper to the vegetable mixture.
- Cook over low heat for 3 to 5 minutes. Transfer the cooked vegetables to a large bowl.
- Add the cooked pasta and shredded mozzarella cheese.
- Toss gently to mix.
- Spoon the mixture into the prepared baking dish.
- Sprinkle with the grated Parmesan cheese.
- Cover with aluminum foil and bake until the mixture is hot and bubbly, about 30 minutes.
- Remove the aluminum foil after 15 minutes.
- Divide the pasta among warmed individual bowls.
- Serve immediately.

Balsamic Feta Chicken

Ingredients
- 6 chicken breasts, 4 ounces each
- 1/2 cup balsamic vinegar
- 2 tablespoons brown sugar
- 1 tablespoon olive oil
- 1 tablespoon paprika
- 1 teaspoon chopped fresh thyme
- 1/2 teaspoon kosher salt
- 1/4 teaspoon dry mustard
- 6 tablespoons crumbled feta cheese

Directions
- Heat the oven to 375 F.
- Lightly coat a baking sheet or baking dish with cooking spray or olive oil.
- In a medium bowl, combine the chicken breasts, vinegar, brown sugar, oil, paprika, thyme, salt and mustard.
- Using tongs, coat the chicken.
- Marinate the chicken breasts for at least 20 minutes in the refrigerator.
- Place the marinaded chicken breasts on the baking sheet and bake for 15 minutes or

until chicken reaches an internal temperature of 165 F.
- Sprinkle each chicken breast with 1 tablespoon cheese and serve.

Balsamic Roast Chicken

Ingredients
- 1 whole chicken, about 4 pounds
- 1 tablespoon fresh rosemary or 1 teaspoon dried rosemary
- 1 garlic clove
- 1 tablespoon olive oil
- 1/8 teaspoon freshly ground black pepper
- 8 sprigs fresh rosemary
- 1/2 cup balsamic vinegar
- 1 teaspoon brown sugar

Directions
- Heat the oven to 350 F.
- Mince together the rosemary and garlic. Loosen the chicken skin from the flesh, and rub the flesh with olive oil and then the herb mixture.
- Sprinkle with black pepper.

- Put 2 rosemary sprigs into the cavity of the chicken.
- Truss the chicken.
- Place the chicken into a roasting pan and roast for 20 to 25 minutes per pound, about 1-hour and 20 minutes.
- Whole chicken should cook to a minimum internal temperature of 165 F.
- Baste frequently with pan juices.
- When the chicken is browned and the juices run clear, transfer the chicken to a serving platter.
- In a small saucepan, combine the balsamic vinegar and brown sugar.
- Heat until the mixture is warmed and brown sugar dissolves, but don't boil.
- Carve the chicken and remove the skin.
- Top the pieces with the vinegar mixture. Garnish with the remaining rosemary and serve immediately.

Barbecue Chicken Pizza

Ingredients
- 1 cup tomato sauce, no salt added
- One 12-inch thin, whole-grain pizza crust
- 1 green pepper, cut into rings
- 1 tomato, sliced
- 1 cup mushrooms, sliced
- 4 ounces cooked chicken breast, sliced about 1-inch thick, with all visible fat removed
- 4 tablespoons barbecue sauce
- 1 cup shredded, reduced-fat mozzarella cheese (about 4 ounces)

Directions
- Heat the oven to 400 F.
- Spread the sauce evenly over the pizza crust.
- Add the pepper, tomato, mushrooms and chicken.
- Drizzle barbecue sauce over the pizza and top with cheese.
- Bake about 12 to 14 minutes.
- Cut the pizza into 8 slices and serve.

Barbecued Pork Tenderloin

Ingredients
- 2 teaspoons firmly packed brown sugar
- 1 teaspoon ground allspice
- 1 teaspoon ground cinnamon
- 1/2 teaspoon ground ginger
- 1/2 teaspoon onion powder
- 1/2 teaspoon garlic powder
- 1/4 teaspoon cayenne pepper
- 1/8 teaspoon ground cloves
- 3/4 teaspoon salt, divided
- 1/2 teaspoon freshly ground black pepper
- 1 pork tenderloin, about 1 pound, trimmed of visible fat
- 2 teaspoons white vinegar
- 1 1/2 teaspoons dark honey
- 1 teaspoon tomato paste

Directions
- In a small bowl, combine the brown sugar, allspice, cinnamon, ginger, onion powder, garlic powder, cayenne pepper, cloves, 1/2 teaspoon of the salt and the black pepper.

- Rub the spice mixture over the pork and let stand for 15 minutes.
- In another small bowl, combine the vinegar, honey, tomato paste and the remaining 1/4 teaspoon salt.
- Whisk to blend.
- Set aside.
- Prepare a hot fire in a charcoal grill or heat a gas grill or broiler (grill) to medium-high or 400 F.
- Away from the heat source, lightly coat the grill rack or broiler pan with cooking spray.
- Position the cooking rack 4 to 6 inches from the heat source.
- Place the pork on the grill rack or broiler pan.
- Grill or broil at medium-high heat, turning several times, until browned on all sides, 3 to 4 minutes total.
- Remove to a cooler part of the grill or reduce the heat and continue cooking for 14 to 16 minutes.
- Paste with the vinegar-honey glaze and continue cooking until the pork is slightly pink inside and an instant-read

thermometer inserted into the thickest part reads 160 F, 3 to 4 minutes longer.

- Transfer to a cutting board and let cool for 5 minutes before slicing.
- To serve, slice the pork tenderloin roscswise into 16 pieces and arrange on a warmed serving platter, or divide the slices among individual plates.

Almond Crusted Chicken

Ingredients

- 3/4 cup ground almonds
- 1/2 cup all-purpose flour
- 1 teaspoon dry thyme
- 1 teaspoon onion powder
- 1 teaspoon garlic powder
- 1/2 teaspoon salt
- 1/2 teaspoon pepper
- 1/2 cup skim milk
- 4 boneless, skinless, chicken breast, 4 ounces each
- 1 tablespoon olive oil

Directions

- Heat oven to 400 F.
- Lightly coat a baking sheet with cooking spray.
- In a medium bowl, combine the ground almonds, flour, thyme, onion powder, garlic powder, salt and pepper.
- Pour the milk in a separate medium-sized bowl.
- Coat each chicken breast in the almond mixture, then into the milk, and back into the almond mixture, and place on the baking sheet.
- Preheat a nonstick saute pan on medium-high heat, and add the olive oil to the pan.
- Once the pan is hot, place the chicken breasts in the pan and reduce heat to medium.
- Sear the chicken breasts on one side until they are golden brown, then sear on the other side for 1 minute.
- Place chicken back on the greased baking sheet and bake in the oven for about 10 minutes or until the internal temperature reaches 165 F.

6-Grain Hot Cereal

Ingredients
- 1/2 cup uncooked pearl barley
- 1/2 cup uncooked red wheat berries
- 1/2 cup uncooked brown rice
- 1/4 cup uncooked steel cut oats
- 3 tablespoons uncooked quinoa
- 2 tablespoons of flaxseed
- 1/2 teaspoon kosher salt
- 1 1/2 quarts water

Directions
- In a large saucepan, combine the barley, wheat berries, rice, oats, quinoa, flaxseed and salt.
- Pour water over ingredients, stir and bring to a boil over medium heat.
- Reduce heat to low and simmer for 45 minutes, stirring occasionally.

Barley and Roasted Tomato Risotto

Ingredients

- 10 large plum (Roma) tomatoes, about 2 pounds total weight, peeled and each cut into 4 wedges
- 2 tablespoons extra-virgin olive oil
- 1/2 teaspoon salt, divided
- 1/2 teaspoon freshly ground black pepper, divided
- 4 cups low-sodium vegetable stock or broth
- 3 cups water
- 2 shallots, chopped
- 1/4 cup dry white wine, optional
- 2 cups pearl barley
- 3 tablespoons chopped fresh basil, plus whole leaves for garnish
- 3 tablespoons chopped fresh flat-leaf (Italian) parsley
- 1 1/2 tablespoons chopped fresh thyme
- 1/2 cup grated Parmesan cheese, plus extra ungrated Parmesan for making curls for garnish

Directions

- Heat the oven to 450 F.
- Arrange the tomatoes on a nonstick baking sheet.
- Drizzle with 1 tablespoon of the olive oil and sprinkle with 1/4 teaspoon of the salt and 1/4 teaspoon of the pepper.
- Toss gently to mix.
- Roast until the tomatoes are softened and beginning to brown, 25 to 30 minutes.
- Set aside 16 tomato wedges to use for a garnish.
- In a saucepan, combine the vegetable stock and water and bring to a boil over high heat.
- Reduce the heat to low and keep at a simmer.
- In a large, heavy saucepan, heat the remaining 1 tablespoon olive oil over medium heat.
- Add the chopped shallots and saute until soft and translucent, 2 to 3 minutes.
- Stir in the white wine, if using, and cook until most of the liquid evaporates, 2 to 3 minutes.

- Stir in the barley and cook, stirring, for 1 minute.
- Stir in 1/2 cup of the stock mixture and cook until the liquid is completely absorbed, stirring occasionally.
- Continue stirring in the stock mixture in 1/2-cup increments, cooking each time until the liquid is absorbed before adding more, until the barley is tender, 45 to 50 minutes total.
- Remove from the heat and fold in the tomatoes, chopped basil, parsley, thyme and grated cheese.
- Add the remaining 1/4 teaspoon salt and 1/4 teaspoon pepper and stir to combine.
- Divide the risotto among warmed individual shallow bowls.
- Garnish with the reserved roasted tomato wedges and the whole basil leaves.
- Using a vegetable peeler, cut a curl or two of Parmesan cheese for topping each serving.

Bean Saled with Balsamic Vinaigrette

Ingredients
For the vinaigrette:
- 2 tablespoons balsamic vinegar
- 1/3 cup fresh parsley, chopped
- 4 garlic cloves, finely chopped
- Ground black pepper, to taste
- 1/4 cup extra-virgin olive oil

For the salad:
- 1 can (15 ounces) low-sodium garbanzo beans, rinsed and drained
- 1 can (15 ounces) low-sodium black beans, rinsed and drained
- 1 medium red onion, diced
- 6 lettuce leaves
- 1/2 cup celery, finely chopped

Directions
- To make the vinaigrette, in a small bowl, whisk together the balsamic vinegar, parsley, garlic and pepper.
- While whisking, slowly add the olive oil. Set aside.

- In a large bowl, combine the beans and onion.
- Pour the vinaigrette over the mixture and toss gently to mix well and coat evenly.
- Cover and refrigerate until served.
- To serve, put 1 lettuce leaf on each plate.
- Divide the salad among the individual plates and garnish with chopped celery.
- Serve immediately.

Beef and Vegetable Kebabs

Ingredients
- 1/2 cup brown rice
- 2 cups water
- 4 ounces top sirloin (choice)
- 1 tablespoon fat-free Italian dressing
- 1 green pepper, seeded and cut into 4 pieces
- 4 cherry tomatoes
- 1 small onion, cut into 4 wedges
- 2 wooden skewers, soaked in water for 30 minutes, or metal skewers

Directions

- In a saucepan over high heat, combine the rice and water.
- Bring to a boil.
- Reduce the heat to low, cover and simmer until the water is absorbed and the rice is tender, about 30 to 45 minutes.
- Add more water if necessary to keep the rice from drying out. Transfer to a small bowl to keep warm.
- Cut the meat into 4 equal portions.
- Put the meat in a small bowl and pour Italian dressing over the top.
- Rub the dressing into each piece.
- Cover and place in the refrigerator for at least 20 minutes to marinate, turning as needed.
- Prepare a hot fire in a charcoal grill or heat a gas grill or a broiler.
- Away from the heat source, lightly coat the grill rack or broiler pan with cooking spray.
- Position the cooking rack 4 to 6 inches from the heat source.
- Thread 2 cubes of meat, 2 green pepper pieces, 2 cherry tomatoes and 2 onion wedges onto each skewer.

- Place the kebabs on the grill rack or broiler pan.
- Grill or broil the kebabs for about 5 to 10 minutes, turning as needed.
- Divide the rice onto individual plates.
- Top with 1 kebab and serve immediately.

Beef and Vegetable Stew

Ingredients
- 1 pound beef round steak
- 2 teaspoons canola oil
- 2 cups diced yellow onions
- 1 cup diced celery
- 1 cup diced Roma tomatoes
- 1/2 cup diced sweet potato
- 1/2 cup diced white potato with skin
- 1/2 cup diced mushrooms
- 1 cup diced carrot
- 4 cloves of garlic, chopped
- 1 cup chopped kale
- 1/4 cup uncooked barley
- 1/4 cup red wine vinegar
- 1 teaspoon balsamic vinegar
- 3 cups low-sodium vegetable or beef stock

- 1 teaspoon dried sage, crushed
- 1 teaspoon minced fresh thyme
- 1 tablespoon minced fresh parsley
- 1 tablespoon dried oregano
- 1 teaspoon dried rosemary, minced
- Black pepper, to taste

Directions
- Heat grill or broiler (medium heat).
- Trim fat and gristle from steak.
- Grill or broil steak 12 to 14 minutes, turning once.
- Don't overcook.
- Remove from heat and let rest while preparing vegetables.
- In a large stock pot, saute vegetables in oil over medium-high heat until lightly brown, about 10 minutes.
- Add barley and cook an additional 5 minutes.
- Pat steak dry with paper towels.
- Cut into half-inch pieces and add to pot.
- Then add vinegars, stock, herbs and spices.
- Bring to a boil and simmer 1 hour, until barley is cooked and stew has thickened considerably.

Beef Fajitas

Ingredients
- 1 tablespoon chili powder
- 1/2 teaspoon ground oregano
- 1/2 teaspoon paprika
- 1/4 teaspoon garlic powder
- 1/8 teaspoon salt
- Ground black pepper, to taste
- 12 ounces beef sirloin, select grade, cut into strips 1/2 inch wide and 2 inches long
- 1 red onion, cut into strips
- 1 green bell pepper, cut into strips
- 4 whole-wheat tortillas, about 8 inches in diameter, warmed in the microwave
- 1/4 cup shredded sharp cheddar cheese
- 2 medium tomatoes, diced
- 2 cups shredded lettuce
- 1/2 cup salsa

Directions
- In a small bowl, stir together the chili powder, oregano, paprika, garlic powder, salt and pepper.

- Dredge the sirloin pieces in the seasonings, coating completely.
- In a nonstick frying pan, cook the sirloin strips over medium heat until slightly pink, about 8 minutes.
- Add the onion and green pepper strips and saute until the vegetables are tender, about 5 minutes.
- To serve, spread an equal amount of the meat and vegetable mixture on each tortilla.
- Top each with 1 tablespoon cheese, 1/4 of the diced tomatoes, 1/2 cup shredded lettuce and 2 tablespoons salsa.
- Fold both sides of each tortilla up over the filling, and then roll to close.
- Serve immediately.

Beef Stew with Fennel and Shallots

Ingredients
- 3 tablespoons all-purpose (plain) flour
- 1 pound boneless lean beef stew meat, trimmed of visible fat and cut into 1 1/2-inch cubes

- 2 tablespoons olive oil or canola oil
- 1/2 fennel bulb, trimmed and thinly sliced vertically
- 3 large shallots, chopped (about 3 tablespoons)
- 3/4 teaspoon ground black pepper, divided
- 2 fresh thyme sprigs
- 1 bay leaf
- 3 cups no-salt-added vegetable stock or broth
- 1/2 cup red wine, optional (not included in analysis)
- 4 large carrots, peeled and cut into 1-inch chunks
- 4 large red-skinned or white potatoes, peeled and cut into 1-inch chunks
- 18 small boiling onions, about 10 ounces total weight, halved crosswise
- 3 portobello mushrooms, brushed clean and cut into 1-inch chunks
- 1/3 cup finely chopped fresh flat-leaf (Italian) parsley

Directions
- Place the flour on a plate.

- Dredge the beef cubes in the flour. In a large, heavy saucepan, heat the oil over medium heat.
- Add the beef and cook, turning as needed, until browned on all sides, about 5 minutes.
- Remove the beef from the pan with a slotted spoon and set aside.
- Add the fennel and shallots to the pan over medium heat and saute until softened and lightly golden, 7 to 8 minutes.
- Add 1/4 teaspoon pepper, thyme sprigs and bay leaf. Saute for 1 minute.
- Return the beef to the pan and add the vegetable stock and the wine, if using.
- Bring to a boil, then reduce the heat to low, cover and simmer gently until the meat is tender, 40 to 45 minutes.
- Add the carrots, potatoes, onions and mushrooms.
- The liquid will not cover the vegetables completely, but more liquid will accumulate as the mushrooms soften.
- Simmer gently until the vegetables are tender, about 30 minutes longer.
- Discard the thyme sprigs and bay leaf.

- Stir in the parsley and remaining 1/2 teaspoon pepper.
- Ladle into warmed individual bowls and serve immediately.

Beef Stroganoff

Ingredients
- 1/2 cup chopped onion
- 1/2 pound boneless beef round steak, cut 3/4-inch thick, all fat removed
- 4 cups uncooked yolkless egg noodles
- 1/2 can fat-free cream of mushroom soup (undiluted)
- 1/2 cup of water
- 1 tablespoon all-purpose (plain) flour
- 1/2 teaspoon paprika
- 1/2 cup fat-free sour cream

Directions
- In a nonstick frying pan, saute the onions over medium heat until they're translucent, about 5 minutes.

- Add the beef and continue to cook for another 5 minutes or until the beef is tender and browned throughout.
- Drain well and set aside.
- Fill a large pot 3/4 full with water and bring to a boil.
- Add the noodles and cook until al dente (tender), 10 to 12 minutes, or according to the package directions.
- Drain the pasta thoroughly.
- In a saucepan, whisk together the soup, water and flour over medium heat.
- Stir until the sauce thickens, about 5 minutes.
- Add the soup mixture and paprika to the beef in the frying pan.
- Over medium heat, stir the mixture until warmed through.
- Remove from heat and add the sour cream.
- Stir until combined.
- To serve, divide the pasta among the plates.
- Top with the beef mixture and serve immediately.

Black Bean Burgers with Chipotle Ketchup

Ingredients

- 1 1/4 cups dried black beans, picked over and rinsed, soaked overnight, and drained
- 3 cups water
- 1 bay leaf
- 2 plum (Roma) tomatoes, peeled and seeded, then diced
- 1 yellow onion, chopped
- 4 cloves garlic, minced
- 1 tablespoon tomato paste
- 1 tablespoon wine vinegar
- 1 chipotle chili in adobo sauce, minced
- 1 3/4 teaspoons ground cumin
- 1/2 teaspoon salt
- 1 1/2 tablespoons canola oil
- 1/2 red bell pepper (capsicum), seeded and chopped
- 1/2 cup cooked brown rice
- 1/4 cup chopped pecans
- 1 green (spring) onion, thinly sliced
- 1 egg, lightly beaten
- 3/4 cup fresh whole-grain bread crumbs
- 6 whole-grain hamburger buns

- 6 slices tomato
- 6 slices red onion
- 3 bibb lettuce leaves, halved

Directions
- In a large saucepan over high heat, combine the beans, water and bay leaf.
- Bring to a boil.
- Reduce the heat to low, cover partially, and simmer until the beans are tender, 60 to 70 minutes.
- Drain and discard the bay leaf.
- While the beans are cooking, make the chipotle ketchup.
- In a small saucepan over medium-high heat, combine the tomatoes, half the yellow onion, half the garlic, the tomato paste, vinegar, chipotle chili, 3/4 teaspoon of the cumin and 1/4 teaspoon of the salt.
- Bring the mixture to a boil.
- Reduce the heat to medium and simmer uncovered, stirring occasionally, until the liquid is reduced and the mixture is a thick sauce, about 5 minutes.
- Set aside to cool.

- In a frying pan, heat 1/2 tablespoon of the canola oil over medium heat.
- Add the remaining yellow onion and saute until soft and translucent, about 4 minutes.
- Add the bell pepper and the remaining garlic and saute until they begin to soften, about 3 minutes. Stir in 1/4 teaspoon of the salt, transfer the mixture to a bowl and let cool.
- Set the pan aside.
- In a food processor, combine the drained beans, onion mixture, brown rice, pecans, green onion and the remaining 1 teaspoon cumin.
- Pulse several times until the mixture is coarsely pureed.
- Fold in the beaten egg and bread crumbs.
- Form the mixture into 6 patties, each about 3/4-inch thick.
- In the same pan used for the onion mixture, heat the remaining 1 tablespoon canola oil over medium-high heat.
- Add the patties and cook, turning once, until nicely browned on both sides and heated through, 7 to 9 minutes total.

- Serve each burger on a bun topped with 1 tomato slice, 1 onion slice, 1/2 lettuce leaf and a dollop of the ketchup.

CONCLUSION

It is generally recommended to consult with a healthcare provider, registered dietician, or even a certified health coach prior to beginning any type of weight management plan. It is also important to ensure you are following the official Mayo Clinic Diet, as many phony versions, often promoting unhealthy habits, are in circulation.

Remember, following a long-term or short-term diet may not be necessary for you and many diets out there simply don't work, especially long-term. While we do not endorse fad diet trends or unsustainable weight loss methods, we present the facts so you can make an informed decision that works best for your nutritional needs, genetic blueprint, budget, and goals.

If your goal is weight loss, remember that losing weight isn't necessarily the same as being your healthiest self, and there are many other ways to pursue health. Exercise, sleep, and other lifestyle factors also play a major role in your overall health. The best diet is always the one that is balanced and fits your lifestyle.

Made in the USA
Monee, IL
20 May 2024

58637583R00049